PIANO ACCOMPANIMENT (+ OBOE PART)

GABRIEL'S OBOE

FROM THE MOTION PICTURE

THE MISSION

MUSIC BY
ENNIO MORRICONE

CHRYSALIS

EXCLUSIVELY DISTRIBUTED BY

HAL•LEONARD®
CORPORATION

7777 W. BLUEMOUND RD. P.O. BOX 13819 MILWAUKEE, WI 53213

GABRIEL'S OBOE

MUSIC BY ENNIO MORRICONE

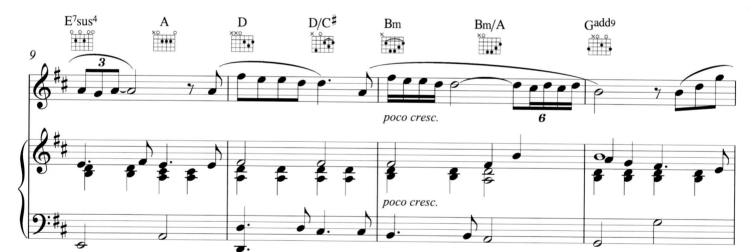

PIANO SOLO

GABRIEL'S OBOE

MUSIC BY ENNIO MORRICONE

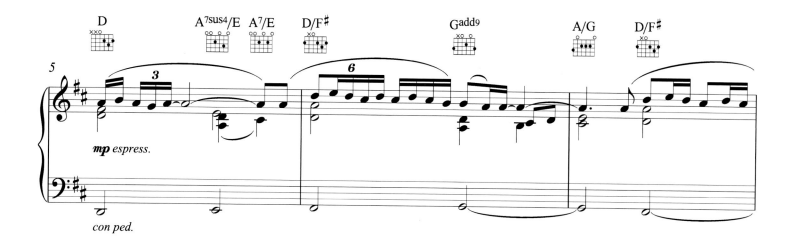

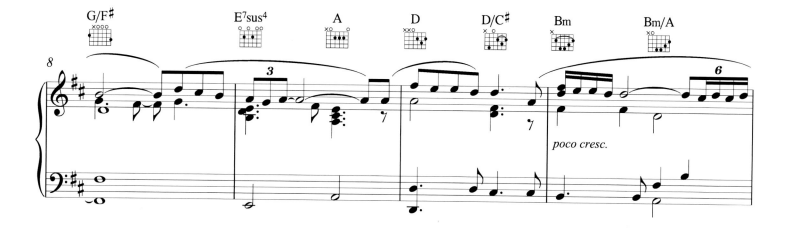

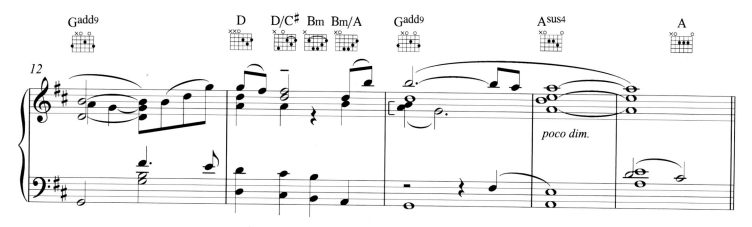

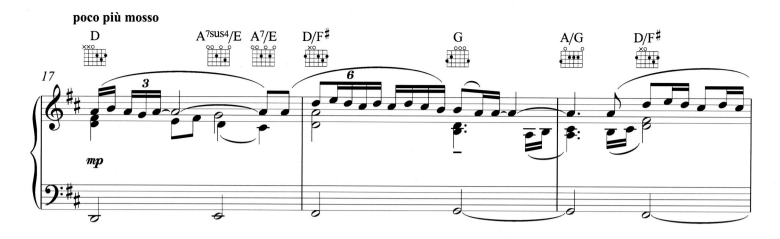

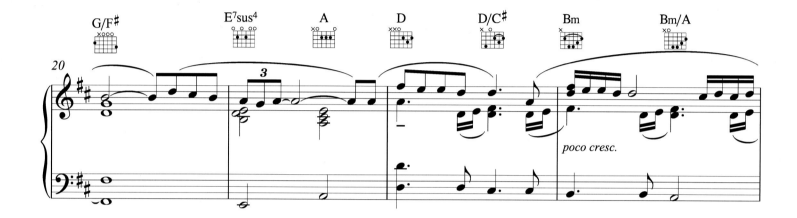

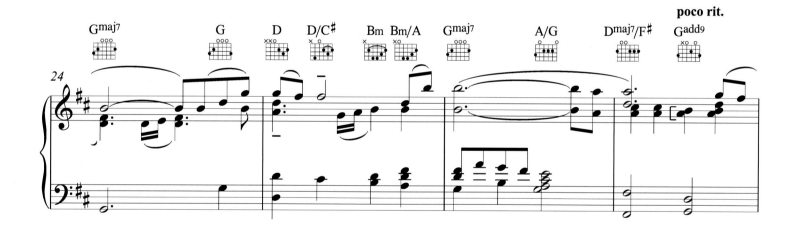

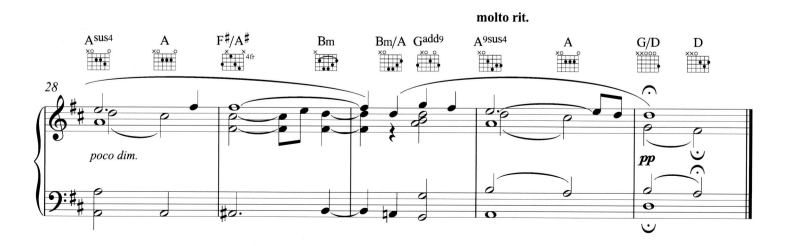

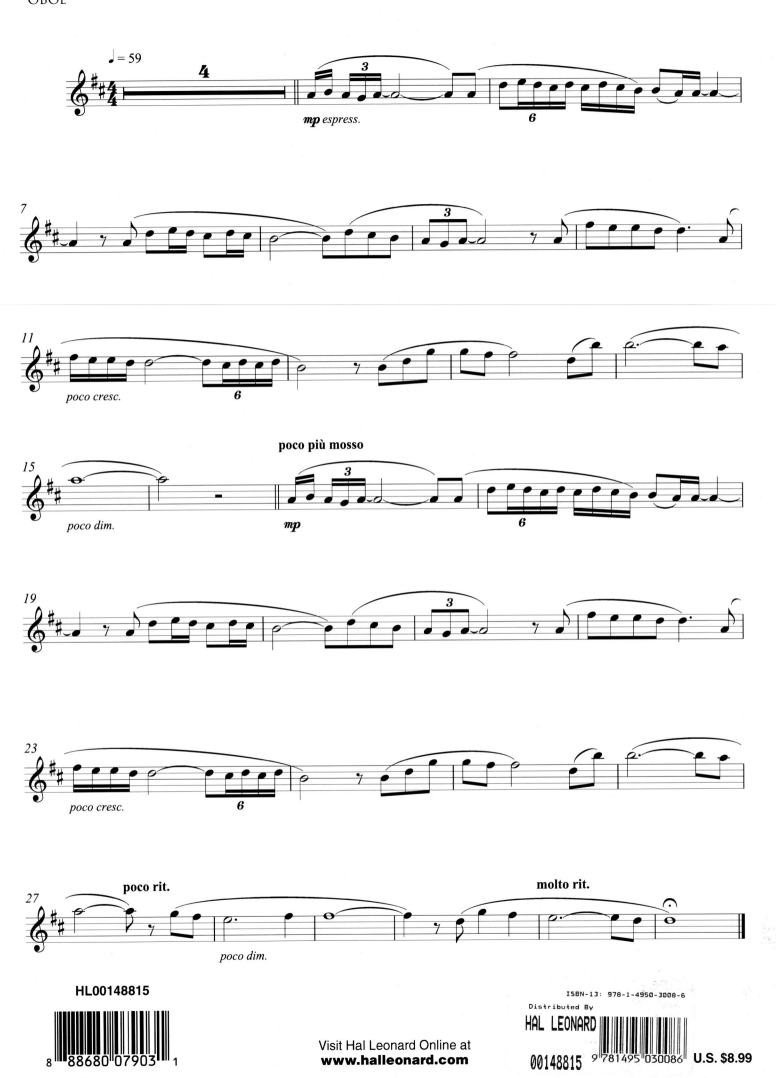

HL00148815

ISBN-13: 978-1-4950-3008-6

Distributed By

HAL LEONARD

8 88680 07903 1

00148815   9 781495 030086   U.S. $8.99